Prayers and Graces

Prayers and Graces

COMPILED BY GAIL HARVEY

JellyBean Press
NEW YORK · AVENEL

For Augie and Emily

Introduction and Compilation
Copyright © 1993 by Random House Value Publishing, Inc.

First published in 1993 by JellyBean Press,
distributed by Random House Value Publishing, Inc.,
40 Engelhard Avenue
Avenel, New Jersey 07001

Designed by Liz Trovato

Manufactured in the United States

Library of Congress Cataloging-in-Publication Data

Prayers and graces / compiled by Gail Harvey, illustrated by
Jessie Willcox Smith, Millicent Sowerby, Margaret Tarrant.
p.   cm.
Summary: An illustrated collection of familiar prayers
written for children.
ISBN 0-517-09276-X
1. Children—Prayer-books and devotions—English.
I. Smith, Jessie Willcox, 1863–1935, ill.   II. Sowerby,
Millicent, ill.
III. Tarrant, Margaret, 1888–1969, ill.
BV4571.2.P73   1993
242'.82—dc20   92-39152
CIP
AC

10 9 8 7 6 5

Contents

Introduction

The prayers and graces in this collection are just right for the different times when it helps to talk to God. There are prayers to give thanks before starting the day or before sitting down to eat with friends and family. There are prayers for bedtime and even a special prayer for a birthday. Some of these prayers give thanks to God for His goodness, others praise Him for His greatness, and some ask His forgiveness.

The prayers we learn as children stay with us throughout our lives and their meaning becomes deeper and richer as time goes by. *Prayers and Graces* includes some of the loveliest prayers ever written in the English language for children. It is a collection that provides the opportunity to help girls and boys of all ages to pray in a direct and natural way.

There are many short and simple prayers that will please small children, who will immediately understand them and will quickly memorize the words. Older children will appreciate the well-known prayers that are included, like the Twenty-Third Psalm and The Lord's Prayer, as well as the beautiful poems by such famous writers as Robert Louis Stevenson, Elizabeth Barrett Browning, Charles Wesley, Ralph Waldo Emerson, William Blake, and Samuel Taylor Coleridge.

The prayers and graces are complemented by charming illustrations by such notable artists as Jessie Willcox Smith, Millicent Sowerby, Margaret W. Tarrant, and Charles Robinson.

It is hoped that this lovely book will be welcomed by adults who will remember the prayers from their own childhoods and will be treasured by children who will cherish for a lifetime their introduction to prayer.

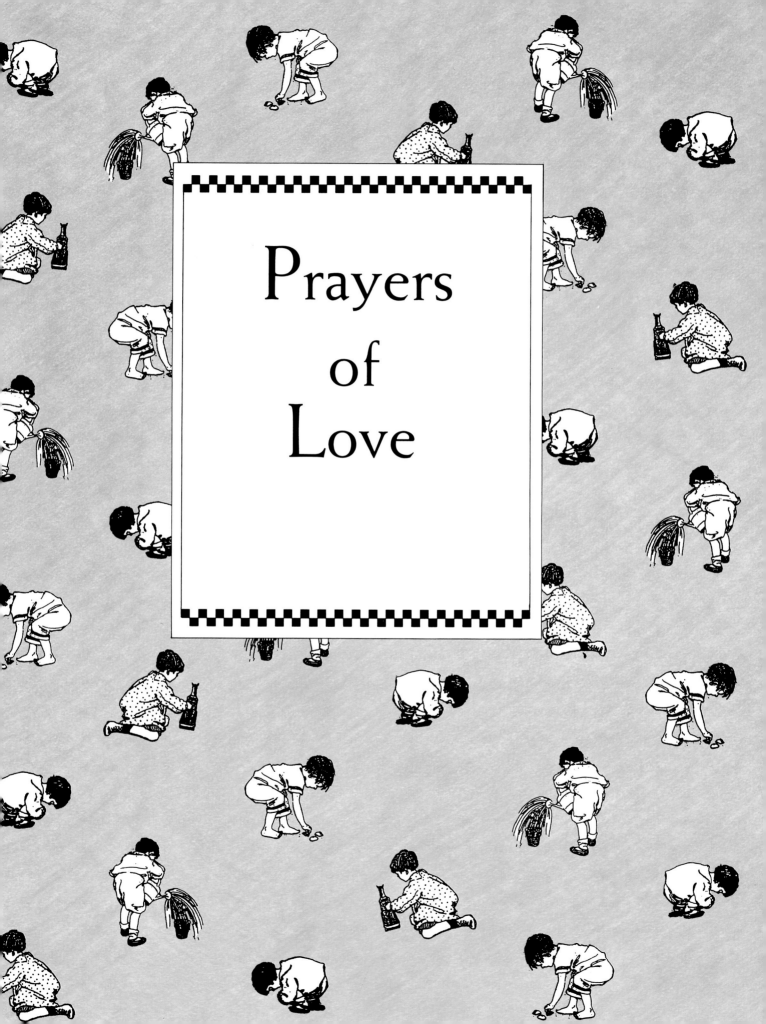

Prayers
of
Love

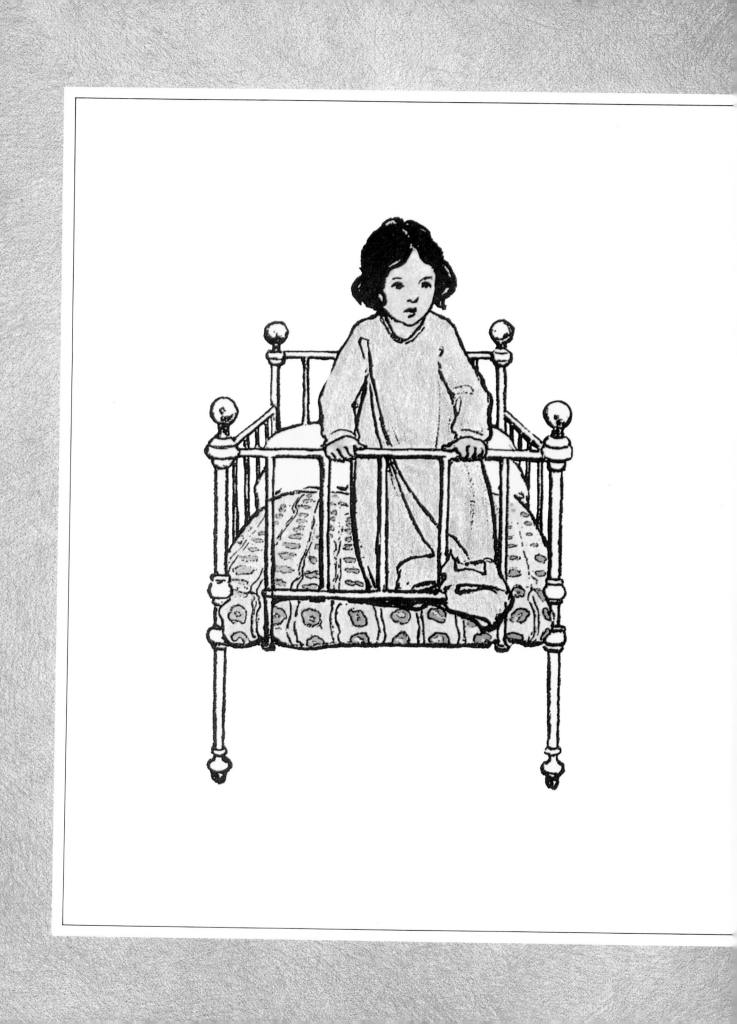

Now I Wake

Now I wake and see the light,
Thy love was with me through the night;
To Thee I speak again and pray
That Thou wilt lead me all the day.
Amen.

I thank Thee, Lord, for quiet rest,
　　And for Thy care of me:
Oh! let me through this day be blest,
　　And kept from harm by Thee.

Oh, let me love Thee! kind Thou art
　　To children such as I;
Give me a gentle, holy heart,
　　Be Thou my Friend on high.

Help me to please my parents dear,
　　And do whate'er they tell;
Bless all my friends, both far and near,
　　And keep them safe and well.
　　　　　　　　MARY LUNDIE DUNCAN

A Child's Prayer

Lord, teach a little child to pray,
    And oh, accept my prayer;
Thou canst hear all the words I say,
    For Thou art everywhere.
Amen.

A Prayer

Father, we thank Thee for the night
And for the pleasant morning light,
For rest and food and loving care,
And all that makes the world so fair.
Help us to do the thing we should,
To be to others kind and good,
In all we do, in all we say,
To grow more loving every day.

Now, before I run to play,
   Let me not forget to pray
To God Who kept me through the night
   And waked me with the morning light.

Help me, Lord, to love Thee more
   Than I ever loved before,
In my work and in my play,
   Be Thou with me through the day.
Amen.

Morning Hymn

Now the sun is in the skies,
From my bed again I rise;
Christ, Thou never-setting Sun,
Shine on me, Thy little one.

Watch me through the coming day,
Guard me in my work and play;
Christ my Master, Christ the Child,
Make me like Thee, Jesu mild.

Christ, Almighty King above,
Thee I pray for all I love;
Christ, who lovest more than I,
Help them from Thy throne on high.

Christ, of Mary born for me,
To Thy name I bow the knee;
Savior, bring us, by Thy grace,
To Thy happy dwelling-place.

R. F. LITTLEDALF

For This New Morning

For this new morning and its light,
For rest and shelter of the night,
For health and food, for love and friends,
For every gift His goodness sends
We thank Thee, gracious Lord.
Amen.

Heavenly Father, Hear Our Prayer

Heavenly Father, hear our prayer,
Keep us in Thy loving care.
Guard us through the livelong day,
In our work and in our play.
Keep us pure and sweet and true,
In everything we say and do.
Amen.

Lord of the
Loving Heart

Lord of the loving heart,
May mine be loving too.
Lord of the gentle hands,
May mine be gentle too.
Lord of the willing feet,
May mine be willing too.
So may I grow more like thee
In all I say and do.

The Lord's Prayer

Our Father who art in heaven
Hallowed be thy name.
Thy kingdom come;
Thy will be done
On earth as it is in heaven.
Give us this day our daily bread,
And forgive us our trespasses,
As we forgive those who trespass against us.
And lead us not into temptation,
But deliver us from evil:
For thine is the kingdom,
And the power, and the glory,
Forever.
Amen

God, Who Hath Made the Daisies

God, who hath made the daisies
    And ev'ry lovely thing,
He will accept our praises,
    And hearken while we sing.
He says though we are simple,
    Though ignorant we be,
"Suffer the little children,
    And let them come to Me."

Though we are young and simple,
    In praise we may be bold;
The children in the temple
    He heard in days of old.
And if our hearts are humble,
    He says to you and me,
"Suffer the little children,
    And let them come to Me."

He sees the bird that wingeth
    Its way o'er earth and sky;
He hears the lark that singeth
    Up in the heaven so high;
But sees the heart's low breathings,
    And says (well pleased to see),
"Suffer the little children,
    And let them come to Me."

Therefore we will come near Him,
    And solemnly we'll sing;
No cause to shrink or fear Him,
    We'll make our voices ring;
For in our temple speaking,
    He says to you and me,
"Suffer the little children,
    And let them come to Me."

E. P. HOOD

A Child's Hymn

God, make my life a little light
    Within the world to glow;
A little flame that burneth bright,
    Wherever I may go.

God, make my life a little flower
    That giveth joy to all,
Content to bloom in native bower,
    Although the place be small.

God, make my life a little song
    That comforteth the sad;
That helpeth others to be strong,
    And makes the singer glad.

God, make my life a little staff
    Whereon the weak may rest,
That so what health and strength I have
    May serve my neighbors best.

God, make my life a little hymn
    Of tenderness and praise;
Of faith—that never waxeth dim,
    In all His wondrous ways.
                                    MATILDA B. EDWARDS

Father, I give Thee thanks
that Thou has heard me.
And I know that Thou
hearest me always.
ST. JOHN 11:41–42

The Lord is my shepherd; I shall not want. He maketh me to lie down in green pastures. He leadeth me beside the still waters. He restoreth my soul. He leadeth me in the paths of righteousness for his name's sake. Yea, though I walk through the valley of the shadow of death, I will fear no evil; for thou art with me; thy rod and thy staff, they comfort me. Thou preparest a table before me in the presence of mine enemies; thou anointest my head with oil; my cup runneth over. Surely goodness and mercy shall follow me all the days of my life; and I will dwell in the house of the Lord forever.

PSALM 23

Dear Father,
    Hear and bless
Thy beasts
    And singing birds:
And guard with tenderness
    Small things
That have no words.

It is a good thing
    to give praise
    to the Lord:
And to sing
    to Thy name,
    O most High.
PSALM 91

Father, help Thy little child;
Make me truthful, good, and mild,
Kind, obedient, modest, meek,
Mindful of the words I speak;
What is right may I pursue;
What is wrong refuse to do;
What is evil seek to shun;
This I ask through Christ, Thy Son.
Amen.

Margaret W. Tarrant

Can a little child like me
Thank the Father fittingly?
Yes, oh, yes—be good and true,
Patient, kind in all you do,
Love the Lord and do your part,
Learn to say with all your heart:
"Father, we thank Thee;
Father in heaven, we thank Thee."
MARY MAPES DODGE

Father, We Thank Thee

For flowers that bloom about our feet,
   Father, we thank Thee,
For tender grass so fresh and sweet,
   Father, we thank Thee,
For song of bird and hum of bee,
For all things fair we hear or see,
Father in heaven, we thank Thee.

For blue of stream and blue of sky,
   Father, we thank Thee,
For pleasant shade of branches high,
   Father, we thank Thee,
For fragrant air and cooling breeze,
For beauty of the blooming trees,
Father in heaven, we thank Thee.

For this new morning with its light,
   Father, we thank Thee,
For rest and shelter of the night,
   Father, we thank Thee,
For health and food, for love and friends,
For everything thy goodness sends,
Father in heaven, we thank Thee.

RALPH WALDO EMERSON

All Things Bright and Beautiful

All things bright and beautiful,
  All creatures, great and small,
All things wise and wonderful,
  The Lord God made them all.

Each little flower that opens,
  Each little bird that sings,
He made their glowing colors,
  He made their tiny wings;

The rich man in his castle,
  The poor man at his gate,
God made them, high or lowly,
  And order'd their estate.

The purple-headed mountain,
  The river running by,
The sunset and the morning
  That brightens up the sky;

The cold wind in the winter,
  The pleasant summer sun,
The ripe fruits in the garden—
  He made them every one.

The tall trees in the greenwood,
  The meadows where we play,
The rushes by the water
  We gather every day.

He gave us eyes to see them,
  And lips that we might tell
How great is God Almighty
  Who has made all things well!
                    CECIL FRANCES ALEXANDER

A Boy's Prayer

God who created me
   Nimble and light of limb,
In three elements free,
   To run, to ride, to swim:
   Not when the sense is dim,
But now from the heart of joy,
   I would remember Him:
Take the thanks of a boy.

H. C. Beeching

The Lamb

Little lamb, who made thee?
Dost thou know who made thee,
Gave thee life, and bade thee feed
By the stream and o'er the mead;
Gave thee clothing of delight,
Softest clothing, woolly, bright;
Gave thee such a tender voice,
Making all the vales rejoice?
　　Little lamb, who made thee?
　　Dost thou know who made thee?

Little lamb, I'll tell thee;
Little lamb, I'll tell thee;
He is callèd by thy name,
For He calls Himself a lamb;
He is meek and He is mild,
He became a little child.
I a child and thou a lamb,
We are callèd by His name.
    Little lamb, God bless thee!
    Little lamb, God bless thee!
                    WILLIAM BLAKE

He prayeth well, who loveth well
Both man and bird and beast.
He prayeth best, who loveth best
All things both great and small;
For the dear God who loveth us,
He made and loveth all.

SAMUEL TAYLOR COLERIDGE

A Prayer
for a Birthday

O Jesus, shed Thy tender love
    Upon me, please, today.
On this my birthday give me grace
    My special prayer to say.

Few are my candles, few my years;
    So let my promise be
That all the years that I may live
    I'll love and worship Thee.

Loving Jesus

Loving Jesus, meek and mild,
Look upon a little child!

Make me gentle as Thou art,
Come and live within my heart.

Take my childish hand in Thine,
Guide these little feet of mine.

So shall all my happy days
Sing their pleasant song of praise;

And the world shall always see
Christ, the Holy Child, in me.

CHARLES WESLEY

Graces

At the table, ere we sit,
　We must never Grace omit;
But, for all the good things nigh,
　Thank our Father up on high.

So, a little child, I pray,
    When we work or when we play,
Blessings on this day begun
    For ourselves and everyone;
Amen.

A Child's Grace

God is great and God is good,
And we thank Him for our food;
By His hand we must be fed,
Give us, Lord, our daily bread.
Amen.

BABY'S GRACE

Thank you for the world so sweet,
Thank you for the food we eat,
Thank you for the birds that sing,
Thank you, God, for everything.
                                    E. R. LEATHAM

Bless us, O Lord,
  And these, Thy gifts,
Which we are about to receive
  From Thy bounty,
Through Christ Our Lord.
Amen.

God bless this food,
And bless us all,
And keep us safe,
Whate'er befall.
For Jesus' sake.
Amen.

What God gives and what we take,
'Tis a gift for Christ, His sake;
Be the meal of beans or peas,
God be thanked for those and these;
Have we flesh, or have we fish,
All are fragments from His dish.

ROBERT HERRICK

A Simple Grace

Father, bless the food we take
And bless us all for Jesus' sake.
Amen.

A Grace Before Meals

We thank Thee, Lord, for daily bread
As by Thy hands our souls are fed.
Grant us to grow more like to Thee,
Today and through eternity.
Amen.

Graces Before Meat

I

Bless these Thy gifts, most gracious God,
    From whom all goodness springs;
Make clean our hearts and feed our souls
    With good and joyful things.

II

Pray we to God, the Almighty Lord,
That sendeth food to beasts and men,
To send His blessing on this board,
To feed us now and ever.
Amen.

Thou openest Thy hand, O Lord,
The earth is filled with good;
Teach us with grateful hearts to take
From Thee our daily food.

A Thought

It is very nice to think
The world is full of meat and drink,
With little children saying grace
In every Christian kind of place.
ROBERT LOUIS STEVENSON

A Thanksgiving

For food and all Thy gifts of love,
  We give Thee thanks and praise.
Look down, O Father, from above,
  And bless us all our days.
Amen.

Prayers
for
Bedtime

The Eyes of God

God watches o'er us all the day,
At home, at school, and at our play;
And when the sun has left the skies
He watches with a million eyes.

GABRIEL SETOUN

Bedtime

Before the last good night is said
    And ere he tumbles into bed,
A little child should have a care
    And not forget to say a prayer
To God the Father who, with love,
    Looks down on children from above
To guard them always, night and day,
    And guide their feet upon the way.

I Thank Thee

I thank Thee for the love so true
That watched o'er me the long day through
Dear Savior, keep me through the night
And wake me with the morning's light.
Amen.

Through the Night

Loving Father, put away
All the wrong I've done today;
Make me sorry, true, and good;
Make me love Thee as I should;
Make me feel by day and night
I am ever in Thy sight.

Heavenly Father, hear my prayer;
Take Thy child into Thy care;
Let Thy angels pure and bright
Watch around me through the night.
Amen.

Good Night Prayer
for a Little Child

Father, unto Thee I pray,

Thou hast guarded me all day;

Safe I am while in Thy sight,

Safely let me sleep tonight.

Bless my friends, the whole world bless,

Help me to learn helpfulness;

Keep me ever in Thy sight:

So to all I say good night.

HENRY JOHNSTONE

Good night! Good night!
Far flies the light;
But still God's love
Shall flame above,
Making all bright.
Good night! Good night!

A Child's Thought of God

They say that God lives very high!
    But if you look above the pines
You cannot see our God. And why?

And if you dig down in the mines
    You never see Him in the gold,
Though from Him all that's glory
        shines.

God is so good, He wears a fold
    Of heaven and earth across His
        face—
Like secrets kept, for love untold.

But still I feel that His embrace
    Slides down by thrills, through all
        things made,
Through sight and sound of every
        place:

As if my tender mother laid
    On my shut lids, her kisses'
        pressure,
Half-waking me at night and said,
    "Who kissed you through the dark,
        dear guesser?"
        ELIZABETH BARRETT BROWNING

I have two fathers, people say—
One for the night and one for day.

The one who talks and plays with me
And one I cannot hear or see.

I send my prayers away on high
To where He lives behind the sky.

And then I listen in my bed
To hear my other father's tread.

He comes when things are growing dim
And brings the candlestick with him.

He makes my bedroom full of light
And answers when I say good night.

Child's Evening Prayer

Ere on my bed my limbs I lay,
God grant me grace my prayers to
    say!
O God, preserve my mother dear
In health and strength for many a
    year.
And O preserve my father too,
And may I pay him reverence due;
And may I my best thoughts employ
To be my parents' hope and joy!
And O preserve my brothers both
From evil doings and from sloth,
And may we always love each other,
Our friends, our father, and our
    mother!
And still, O Lord, to me impart
An innocent and grateful heart,
That after my last sleep I may
Awake to Thy eternal day.
Amen.

SAMUEL TAYLOR COLERIDGE

Now I lay me down to sleep,
I pray Thee, Lord, my soul to keep;
Thy love stay with me through the night
And wake me with the morning light.
Amen.

Jesus, tender Shepherd, hear me;
   Bless thy little lamb tonight;
Through the darkness be Thou near me,
   Keep me safe till morning light.

All this day thy hand has led me,
   And I thank thee for thy care;
Thou has warmed me, clothed and fed me;
   Listen to my evening prayer!

Let my sins be all forgiven;
   Bless the friends I love so well:
Take us all at last to heaven,
   Happy there with thee to dwell.

MARY DUNCAN

Prayer at Bedtime

Matthew, Mark, Luke, and John
Bless the bed that I lie on.
Four corners to my bed,
Four angels there be spread:
One at the head, one at the feet,
And two to guard me while I sleep.
God within, and God without,
And Jesus Christ all round about;
If any danger come to me,
Sweet Jesus Christ deliver me.
Before I lay me down to sleep
I give my soul to Christ to keep;
And if I die before I wake,
I pray that Christ my soul will take.

Evening Hymn

On the dark hill's western side
The last purple gleam has died,
Twilight to one solemn hue
Changes all, both green and blue.

In the fold and in the nest,
Birds and lambs are gone to rest,
Labor's weary task is o'er,
Closely shut the cottage door.

Savior, ere in sweet repose
I my weary eyelids close,
While my mother through the gloom
Singeth from the outer room;

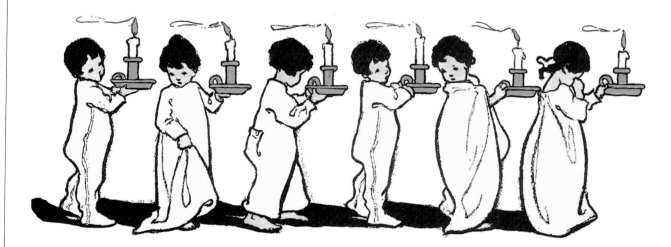

While across the curtain white,
With a dim uncertain light,
On the floor the faint stars shine,
Let my latest thought be Thine.

If my slumbers broken be,
Waking let me think of Thee;
Darkness cannot make me fear,
If I feel that Thou art near.

Happy now I turn to sleep;
Thou wilt watch around me keep,
Him no danger e'er can harm,
Who lies cradled in Thine arm.

CECIL FRANCES ALEXANDER

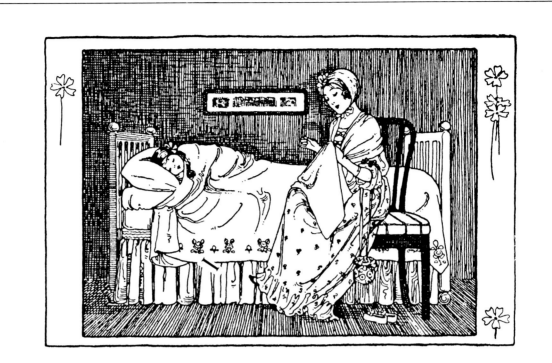

Now the Day is Over

Now the day is over,
  Night is drawing nigh,
Shadows of the evening
  Steal across the sky;

Jesus, give the weary
  Calm and sweet repose;
With thy tenderest blessing
  May our eyelids close.

Grant to little children
  Visions bright of thee;
Guard the sailors tossing
  On the deep, blue sea.

Comfort every sufferer
  Watching late in pain;
Those who plan some evil
  From their sins restrain.

Through the long night watches,
  May thine angels spread
Their white wings above me,
  Watching round my bed.

When the morning wakens,
  Then may I arise
Pure, and fresh, and sinless
  In thy holy eyes.
Amen.

SABINE BARING-GOULD

The Good Shepherd

Kind Shepherd, see, Thy little lamb
  Comes very tired to Thee;
O fold me in Thy loving arms,
  And smile on me.

I've wander'd from Thy fold today,
  And could not hear Thee call;
And O! I was not happy then,
  Nor glad at all.

I want, dear Savior, to be good,
  And follow close to Thee,
Through flowery meads and pastures green
  And happy be.

Thou kind, good Shepherd, in Thy fold
  I evermore would keep,
In morning's light or evening's shade,
  And while I sleep.

But now, dear Jesus, let me lay
  My head upon Thy breast;
I am too tired to tell Thee more,
  Thou know'st the rest.

H. P. HAWKINS